D0535139

WE WERE HERE FIRST
THE NATIVE AMERICANS

THE
APACHE
OF THE SOUTHWEST

RUSSELL
ROBERTS

PURPLE TOAD
PUBLISHING

P.O. Box 631
Kennett Square, Pennsylvania 19348
www.purpletoadpublishing.com

WE WERE HERE FIRST
THE NATIVE AMERICANS

The Apache of the Southwest
The Inuit of the Arctic
The Iroquois of the Northeast
The Nez Perce of the Pacific Northwest
The Sioux of the Great Northern Plains

Printing   1   2   3   4   5   6   7   8   9

Publisher's Cataloging-in-Publication Data
Roberts, Russell, 1953–
   The Apache of the Southwest / Russell Roberts
      p. cm. – (We were here first. The Native Americans)
   Includes bibliographic references and index.
ISBN: 978-1-62469-005-1 (library bound)
1. Apache Indians – Juvenile literature.   I. Title.
   E99.A6 R63 2013
   979.0049'725—dc23
                                              2013930979

eBook ISBN: 978-1-62469-016-7

Printed by Lake Book Manufacturing, Chicago, IL

CONTENTS

The Apaches were one of the first tribes to master the use of the horse. Eventually the horse became part of Apache mythology.

CHAPTER 1: CHOOSING LIFE

The hot wind blew across the dry Texas plains, stirring up the flaky brown dirt and sending clouds of it swirling into the air. Occasionally, some dirt blew into the faces of the men and women who were standing and waiting patiently under the blazing sun. Sweat rolled down their faces, but nobody moved or thought to leave. This was a day they would all remember. This was a day that history would remember.

This was the day that life had been chosen instead of death.

It was August 19, 1749. Standing in one of the plazas of the town of Presidio San Antonio de Bexar were four Native American Apache (uh-PAH-chee) chiefs. Behind them were dozens of members of each of their tribes.

Standing across from the natives stood the Spanish. There were soldiers and officers, hot in their itchy uniforrns. There were government officials and priests, their foreheads glistening with sweat. Mixing about were citizens from the small town. All were anxiously awaiting the upcoming ceremony.

Someday San Antonio would be a large city in Texas with over a million people, but that was years in the future. The town

As good as the Apaches were on horseback, the Comanches were better. Eventually the Comanches were able to defeat the Apaches, partly because of their horsemanship.

had just been founded in 1718, and it wasn't very big at all—it had some buildings and a handful of people. Despite its size, on this day it was the most important place in the world for everyone gathered there.

Escaping death had a way of making things important.

For the Apaches, they needed help and support against their dreaded enemy from the North: the Comanches (kuh-MAN-sheez). The Comanche tribe had driven the Apaches from the southern Great Plains (roughly the modern states of Nebraska, Kansas, and Oklahoma), and were now moving into Texas. The Comanches were excellent horsemen—some called them the best in the world—and they made war against the Apaches relentlessly, sweeping down on them like galloping angels of death. The Apaches were good on horseback too—in fact, they were among the first Native American tribes to learn how to ride horses—but they were no match for the Comanches. The Apaches were fierce warriors themselves, but fighting the Comanches was like trying to hold back the rays of the sun. Gradually, most Apaches had been pushed south by the Comanches, out of their lands on the Plains.

Some Apaches fled deep into the Southwest, into areas that would one day be known as the states of New Mexico and Arizona. Other Apaches escaped into northern and central Texas. Here they ran directly into the Spanish, who were expanding their New World civilization

The Lipan Apaches were one group of Apaches that were driven steadily southwest by the Comanches. The Lipans finally settled on the southern Great Plains.

northward from Mexico. The Apaches in Texas fought the Spanish, but it was like being trapped between two giant rocks: The Spanish on one side, and the Comanches on the other.

The Spanish and Apaches had fought many brutal, bloody battles. The Spanish attacked the Apaches, the natives retaliated, and so on and so forth. It was a vicious cycle of fighting and death, in which each side answered the other's attacks with even more savage attacks of their own. There had to be another way, or nobody would be left alive.

An idea had been circulating among Spanish leaders that the way to stop this cycle was to try peace, not war. Early in 1749, Spanish Captain Joseph de Urrutia issued orders that no natives should be killed except in self-defense, and that any captives taken should be well-treated. In February, Urrutia led a force of 200 men from San Antonio to see how this new idea would work. The Spanish captured about 170 Apache men, women, and children, and brought them back to San Antonio. The

Spanish missionaries thought it was their duty to God and king to convert the Apaches to Catholicism. Sometimes the Apaches were sincere in their desire to be converted, and sometimes they just went along with it so that the foreigners would go away.

The Apache were a very family-oriented people. The kidnapping of their women and children by their enemies was one of the reasons they fought so fiercely against them.

men were jailed, but the women and children were split up among settler's homes with strict orders not to harm them. Then the captain sent word to the Apaches: If they would agree to live in peace, the prisoners would be released. In August, word came from the Apaches: Peace.

Because past relations with the natives had been marked by deceit and treachery, the Spanish moved quickly to show the Apaches their sincerity this time. Just outside San Antonio, they built a large hall. The building would not only serve as a place for the Apaches to live in while they came for the peace ceremony, it would also be somewhere safe that the natives could always visit.

In 1936, the Texas Centennial Commission constructed this replica of Presidio (Fort) San Sabá, which was originally built by the Spanish in 1757. Less than one year later, the original fort was burned by enemies of the Spanish and Apaches.

A lone Apache on horseback could mean several things to his anxious enemies. He could be a solitary scout, or he could be one of many other Apaches hidden in the nearby landscape. The wrong guess might mean death.

On August 16, the Spanish and Apaches met and rode into town together. Two chiefs stayed with Urrutia, and two stayed with other city officials. The rest of the natives stayed in the great hall, which was filled with beef, corn, squash, fruit, and other foods.

Early in the morning on August 19, everyone went to the plaza in town and watched as a giant pit was dug in the ground. Weapons of war were put into the pit—a hatchet, a lance, some arrows, and even a live horse. Urrutia and the four chiefs joined hands and circled the pit three times. Then the chiefs did the same with a settler and a missionary. Finally all those present rushed to the giant hole and threw dirt into it until it was filled to the top.[1]

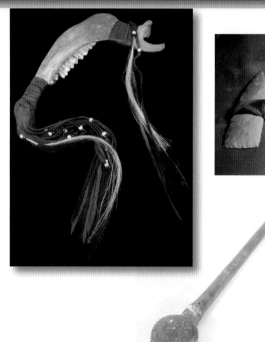

An Apache warrior was especially dangerous in close, hand-to-hand combat. Here, he could use one of several weapons with deadly results, including a club, tomahawk, or animal's jawbone.

The war had been buried. (It is from this that we get the saying "Bury the hatchet," meaning to end acts of war between two or more sides.) Life had been chosen over almost certain death.

The next day the Apaches returned home with their tribe members and the captives the Spanish had released. The Spanish returned to San Antonio. Both sides probably breathed a sigh of relief and enjoyed the restfulness of peace.

For the Apaches, it would be a short rest.

An Apache Creation Story

Many people and cultures have stories about the creation of the world. This is adapted from an Apache story.

A storyteller

In the beginning there was nothing but darkness. From out of the darkness came a thin disk with one yellow side and one white side. In the middle sat a small man with a beard called Creator. He looked into the darkness and light appeared, and also clouds of many colors. Dawn's golden light lit the East, and streaks of fiery red and other colors glowed in the West. Then he created: A shining cloud upon which sat a little girl (known as Girl-Without-Parents), a sun god, and a small boy.

"We can't all stay on this cloud," said Creator. "We must create something else." He then made Tarantula, Lightning-Maker, Wind, Big Dipper, and Lightning-Rumbler.

When all of the gods shook hands, their sweat mixed together. Creator rubbed his hands together, and a brown, bean-sized ball emerged. The four gods took turns kicking it, and each time they did so it grew bigger. Wind went inside the ball and blew it up. Tarantula spun cords on each direction of the ball (north, south, east, and west). The cords then pulled the ball into a giant size until it became the earth.

Creator made four giant, colored posts—blue, yellow, white, and black —to hold Earth steady. Then three creatures were made: Sky-Boy was chief of the Sky-People; Earth-Daughter was in charge of the earth and its crops; and Pollen-Girl was responsible for the health of all the earth people.

A great flood came and covered the entire earth for 12 days. Creator went up on a cloud with 28 helpers to finish working on the sky. Girl-Without-Parents put all the other gods into a large, hollow ball. The ball floated on the water and when the water went down, the ball came to rest on a mountain top. The earth, which had been barren before, was now filled with mountains, hills, and rivers. Lightning-Rumbler was put in charge of the clouds and the water.

The other gods sat on a cloud, which drifted up until it met Creator's cloud. He and his workers had finished the sky. Creator and Girl-Without-Parents made fire. Before walking into the smoke and disappearing, Creator put Girl-Without-Parents in overall charge of the earth. The other gods also vanished into clouds of smoke. The world was ready to be populated by the 28 workers of Creator who remained.

Apaches did not normally see much water in the dry, hot Southwest where many of them lived.

CHAPTER 2: FROM THE NORTH

Most Apaches lived in the dry, hot desert climate of the American Southwest in Arizona, New Mexico, and parts of Texas. (Others lived on the southern Great Plains.) It is strange, then, to realize that the Apaches first came to what is now the United States from Alaska and the Canadian Northwest. Archeological (ar-kee-uh-LAA-jih-kul) evidence (archeology [ar-kee-AHH-luh-jee] is the study of people from the past and their culture) indicates that the group of people known as Apaches came to the region from the North around 1000–1300 CE. They made their way south from there, moving across the eastern portion of the Rocky Mountains until they eventually wound up even farther south. They did not do this quickly; it took centuries for the Apaches to slowly make their way along, living in one place for a while, then moving to another. The Apaches were nomads, meaning that they moved around and never settled in one place for too long.

We know that Apaches came from the Canadian Northwest because they speak the Athapascan (ath-a-PAS-kin) (also known as Athabascan or Athapaskan) language. This language is spoken by people in Northwest Canada.

Archaeologists have different opinions on when the Athapascan-speaking people came to the Southwest. Some think it was as early as the thirteenth century (the 1200s), while others believe it was later, such as the early sixteenth century (the early 1500s). Either way, the Southwest was already home to many other native tribes, including the Hopi, Zuni, Pima, and Havasupai (ha-va-SOO-pie), when the Apaches arrived. It's possible that the word "Apache" comes from the Zuni word "apachu," meaning enemy.[1] Another possibility is the Ute word "Awátche."[2] The Apaches called themselves Inde, or Diné (DIN-air), which means "the people."[3] "Apache" is a name others called them.

One theory about how "Apache" came to refer to the entire group of people is that some members of the tribe initially took over an abandoned pueblo (PWEB-loh) (a pueblo is a type of house) called Navahú. When the Spanish first encountered the Zuni, it sounded like the Zuni were saying, "Apaches de Navahú." So the Spanish began calling those natives Apaches, and that name came to refer to all the natives in the Southwest who were speaking the Athapascan language.[4]

The Apaches de Navahú became known by the Spanish as the Navajo (nah-vuh-HO). Eventually they became the Navaho, which evolved into an entirely separate tribe from the Apaches.[5]

In truth, however, the various tribes called "Apache" were very different peoples. One common way to characterize Apaches is to break them down into six separate tribes: the Lipan and Kiowa-Apache, who lived on the southern Great Plains; the Jicarilla, who lived in the area of the Rio Grande River in northern New Mexico and southeast Colorado; the Chiricahua, who lived in the desert and mountainous areas of southern Arizona and New Mexico; the Mescalero, who lived farthest south in parts of Texas, New Mexico, and northern Mexico; and the Western Apache, who lived in eastern and middle Arizona.

Some researchers think that Apaches in the Southwest first met the Spaniards during Francisco de Coronado's expedition of 1540–1542. Coronado was searching the Southwest for the legendary Golden Cities of Quivira when he came across natives called Querechos in what is today the Texas Panhandle. These natives lived in teepees and followed the buffalo. The encounter between the two was peaceful.

Francisco de Coronado's expedition

The coming of the Spanish would be of great significance to the Apaches. The Spaniards brought metal items with them, and the Apaches, who hadn't seen metal before, quickly adopted it for use as tools, ornaments, and weapons.

More importantly, however, the Spanish brought horses. Although initially the Apaches considered horses as food, just as they did other livestock like cattle and sheep, eventually they realized that horses were valuable in other ways as well. Apaches learned to use horses for hunting, fighting, raiding, and trading.

In the beginning, relations between the Apaches and the Spanish were peaceful. However, that soon changed. The Spanish murdered Apaches and tortured and mistreated them. They repeatedly kidnapped Apache men, women, and children to work as slaves in their precious metal mines, or as servants in the homes and ranches of important people. Naturally, the Apaches fought back.

The Spanish policy in dealing with the native tribes was to pit one against the other; that is, to keep them fighting with each other so that they would not unite and attack the Spanish. As the Spanish viewed the

The Apaches had many enemies, and always had to maintain a sharp lookout for them.

Apaches as the most dangerous of the native tribes, they encouraged other tribes to attack them.

Even when peace attempts were made, they did not survive. A treaty, or agreement, with one group of Apaches did not affect other groups. For example, one Mescalero group might be trading peacefully with the Spanish, while another would be forming a raiding party to steal horses from the Spanish. So the Spanish would accuse the Apaches of breaking the peace treaty, when in fact the group that had made the treaty was still being peaceful. Because they operated under a government of central authority, the Spanish (and later the Americans) couldn't understand why a treaty with one Apache group did not pertain to all Apaches.

In the same manner, the Apaches thought that a treaty with one group of Spaniards applied only to that one, and not all the Spanish. So the Apaches did not see anything wrong with having peaceful relations with one group of Spaniards while attacking another. When this happened, the Spanish would accuse the Apaches of breaking the peace, and war would break out again.

In 1606 the Apaches raided the Spanish settlement of San Gabriel. The Spanish retaliated. The fighting between the two had begun. With some brief interruptions, it would last hundreds of years.

"Excuses to campaign [by the Spanish] against Apaches were seldom wanting after 1601. . . ."[6] wrote researcher Elizabeth John.

The history of the Southwest was about to be written in blood.

The Apaches and Horses

The Apaches were one of the first native tribes to learn how to ride and use horses. As a result, they became the most powerful tribe in the area.

For fighting their enemies, horses allowed the Apaches to swoop down on them, raid and plunder, and then make a speedy get-away. For hunting, the horse made it much easier to track animals over long distances, and it was possible for the hunter to bring back a much greater quantity of meat.

Apache on horseback

Horses made Apache life easier when it came to moving their camp, which as nomads they did quite often. The Apaches had previously used dogs to carry their belongings from place to place on a travois (TRUH-voy), which was a device consisting of two long poles with a platform between them. Each Apache family put their belongings that were to be moved on the platform. (Think of a travois like an open-air suitcase.) Dogs were not that big, and could only pull so much weight. Horses could carry much more weight on a travois, were easier to guide and control than dogs, and could travel greater distances.

Horses became valuable commodities that could be traded for other things the Apaches needed. Apaches found that they could steal horses from the Spanish, then later bring them back and trade them for food, metal, and other items.

The horse became a symbol of wealth and power among the Apaches. A man's prestige within his tribe was measured by the number of horses he owned. A man with many horses was considered a brave warrior, while someone without horses was considered a coward. Boys could not be considered men until they had raided successfully for horses. When an Apache died, his favorite horse was often killed too, so that the two could be together in the next life. Raiding for horses became not just something to do for fun or excitement, but a sacred mission so that Apaches could obtain "the things by which men lived."[7]

The horse became part of the Apaches' sacred myths. They told tales of how their gods gave them the horse. The horse changed life for the Apaches. Little did they know that, before long, the horse would change their lives again, but in a negative way—thanks to the dreaded Comanches, who became the best horseback riders in the world.

Naiche was the youngest son of Cochise, who was one of the greatest Apache chiefs. He had three wives, and along with Geronimo, unsuccessfully went to war to avoid having to live on a reservation. He died in 1919.

CHAPTER 3:
MEN AND WOMEN

For the next several hundred years, the Apaches and the Spanish warred against each other in the Southwest. Who were these fierce, tough, fighting natives whose very name—"Apache"—sent shivers down the spine of every man, woman, and child?

The Apaches were not one large tribe, but a group of many tribes loosely grouped under the name "Apache". So it is difficult to say that certain things applied to all Apaches because what the Kiowa-Apaches followed the Mescalero would not, and so on.

There was not a single chief, or overall leader, of the Apaches. Today, many countries follow central political authority, meaning that when one leader or government does something, it pertains to everyone. However, within a single Apache tribe there were many different bands, which were the tribe's main units. Bands were further divided into local groups. A local group consisted of a chief and his followers, which were usually extended families.

The extended family was the basic unit of life for the Apaches. Their social structure was fluid, meaning that it could easily change. The chief of a local group was more like an advisor or counselor, who made decisions but could not force people to remain with his group if they did not like his decisions.

So, Apache extended families moved among local groups or bands if they chose to do so. The members and numbers of a band or group changed constantly.

The Apache extended family consisted of parents, their unmarried male children, their daughters, and their daughters' husbands and children. Apache families were matrilocal (MAH-truh-loh-kul). This means that newly married couples lived near the wife's family.

To propose marriage, an Apache male would send a gift of horses to a female's family. This showed the family his intentions. However, instead of making the marriage proposal himself, the man asked a friend or relative to do it. If the female ignored the horses or sent them back, that meant she did not accept the proposal. However, if she took the horses to drink water or mixed them in with her father's herd, it meant that the proposal was accepted.

When a man married, he moved from the camp of his parents to that of his wife's parents, and was expected to help take care of them by hunting for food and performing other tasks. The married man obeyed his in-laws as if they were his own parents. If his wife died, the man remained with his wife's parents. Often they would provide him with a new bride. The female had little to do with her husband's parents, but they, too, could provide her with a new groom—usually a cousin or brother—if her husband died.

An extended family did not all live together. Each family unit had its own home, and they camped near each other. Usually several family groups camped together. It helped to have larger numbers for social and ceremonial occasions, such as raiding and hunting. The strongest male member of the various families was the overall leader, but he did not have leadership power and could not force the others to do what he wanted.

Apaches lived in two types of homes. The Kiowas, Jicarillas and some Chiricahuas lived in teepees. A teepee was made of buffalo or another type of animal hide and wrapped around 20-foot-long, wooden poles that were tied together near the top. This was a good type of house for

A teepee was the perfect house for the Apaches, who moved from place to place and needed a dwelling they could put up and take down easily.

people who were nomadic because it could be taken down quickly and moved. Apaches on the Great Plains usually used teepees.

A Spaniard described teepees: "They are made of tanned hides, very bright red and white in color and bell-shaped, with flaps and openings . . . and so large that in the most ordinary ones four different mattresses and beds were easily accommodated."[1]

Many Apaches lived in wickiups (WICK-ee-ups) (also known as wigwams). They were dome-shaped and made with a frame of poles. In hot weather the frame was covered with leafy branches to let air in; and in colder weather animal hides replaced the branches to provide better insulation. Wickiups had a hole in the center for smoke from cooking fires to exit. Built by women in about four hours, the wickiup, like the teepee, could be taken down quickly and moved.[2]

As Coronado said in 1541: "Their tents are in the shape of pavilions. They set them up by means of poles which they carry for the purpose. After driving them in the ground they tie them together at the top."[3]

In camp, male Apaches hunted, raided, and kept a watchful eye out for danger.

Female Apaches did a variety of chores around camp. They tended gardens, gathered seeds and fruit, stored food for times when it was scarce, collected firewood and water, cured and tanned animal hides, and made clothes and other items needed around camp, such as

A woman gathers rushes to make baskets

cooking utensils. Female Apaches took care of children, as well as horses the men brought back to camp.

Because of their knowledge of plants and roots, Apache women were often healers. In his autobiography, *The Life of a Kiowa Apache Indian*, Kiowa Apache Jim Whitewolf relates how he once hurt his right big toe so badly he could barely walk. His mother's aunt brought some white roots to him.

"She chewed some of the root and then rubbed it on my toe," he said. "Then she put some of it [the root] in the fire . . . she took a piece of hide . . . [and] put it on my toe. She prayed as she did."[4] In a few days Jim was perfectly healthy.

The Apache culture greatly valued women. They were respected and protected. A woman's chastity (CHAS-tih-tee) (not having sexual relations before marriage) was strictly enforced. Far from restricting their actions, the Apaches allowed wives to go to war with their husbands. One of the most famous Apache warriors was a woman named Lozen.

The Apaches celebrated life-changing events, because each new life meant the continuation of their people. A female's rite of puberty (PYOO-bur-tee)—the point in her life when she matured from a girl to a childbearing woman—was a major event in Apache life. It was believed that a celebration of the rite of puberty helped strengthen the woman's ability to bear healthy children.

The ritual varied from tribe to tribe. In some tribes, on the first day of the ceremony, the female bathed and dressed in ceremonial clothing. Then she went to a

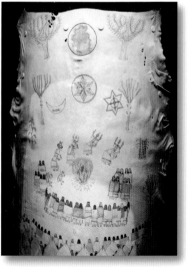

A hide painting of an Apache girl's puberty ceremony.

special structure where she performed ceremonial dances while a male sang creation songs. Females in the Mescalero tribe ran toward the east four times, each time circling a basket filled with special objects. During the evening, masked dancers danced, and later, men and women danced together. In most tribes the ritual would last four days although in the Mescalero tribe it lasted eight. Other tribes had females run in the four directions (north, south, east, west), grind corn, or dance all night and stay up to greet the morning sun. The entire tribe participated in the ceremony as well, by dancing, feasting, and holding contests, such as riding or roping.

In play, children copied what their parents did, such as gathering food and keeping house. Girls had dolls and boys had slings. Both sexes often had pet dogs. Boys and girls frequently swam together, and both sexes developed into excellent swimmers. However, like all children, they were also fond of just playing, using whatever was available. One observer recalled watching Apache children slide down hills using a dried cowhide as a sled.[5]

Boys and girls played together until they were around eight years old. As they grew, older children were discouraged from playing with each other. They were taught not to be alone with each other in homes without parents or grandparents present.

Apache boys trained to be warriors. As small children, boys would run up hills without stopping for breath until they got to the top. Boys bathed each morning in cold water to strengthen their hearts and legs. They ran up to four miles with mouthfuls of water or pebbles so that they were forced to breathe through their noses, which built up their stamina (STAA-mih-nuh) (strength). Other leg strengthening exercises included chasing butterflies and birds and trying to catch them bare-handed. "Your legs are your friends," the older Apaches would tell the young.[6]

At an early age, young Chiricahua boys had their own toy bows and arrows, and they practiced constantly with them. By age six, they were shooting squirrels, birds, and rabbits. When a boy killed his first animal, the custom was for him to eat its heart. Young boys also practiced their aim and accuracy by building fires at night to attract bats, and then throwing their moccasins (MAH-kuh-sinz) (shoes) at the creatures so as to hit them.

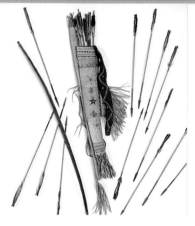

By age seven, Chiricahua boys were learning how to ride horses bareback, or without saddles. Another important part of a boy's training was to learn how to stand

Apache bow and arrows

or crouch absolutely still for minutes at a time. Soldiers chasing Apaches would be amazed at how they could "melt" into a landscape. Undoubtedly, this ability to remain motionless helped account for this.

This training created hard and tough warriors who had few equals in the world. An Apache warrior could travel 40 miles a day by foot, or almost double that on horseback. He lived off the land, eating berries, roots, seeds, even cactus if necessary. The Apaches could read the landscape like other people read books.

An American soldier admired the Apache's ability to understand his surroundings: "Every track in the trail, mark in the grass, scratch on the bark of a tree, explains itself to the . . . [Apache]. He can tell to an hour, almost, when the man or animal making them passed by . . . ."[7]

In the brutal environment of the Southwest, where food and water were scarce, and the only thing plentiful was the hot sun blazing away in the sky, an Apache excelled at survival. He traveled through this unforgiving land as silent as air, dissolved into the landscape as easily as rainwater, and re-emerged with a sudden fury like a thunderstorm. The very name "Apache" struck fear in the hearts of the tribe's enemies because of its fearsome and ghost-like reputation. One American general who fought them called Apaches the "tigers of the human species."[8]

Lozen

One of the most famous Apache warriors of all time was a woman named Lozen. Her life story illustrates how females were treated as equals by the Apaches.

Lozen was a Chiricahua Apache born in the late 1840s. Her brother was Victorio, another famous Apache warrior. In 1877 Victorio and his band left the San Carlos Reservation in Arizona, where conditions were horrible and he could not stand to watch his people die. The band began marauding

Lozen

against the Americans, angry because their homeland in New Mexico had been taken from them. Lozen fought right beside Victorio, and Victorio commented how greatly he depended on his sister.

In one famous episode, the band was being pursued by the Americans when they came upon the Rio Grande River, which was swollen and running very fast and deep. The women and children were scared to try and cross such a raging torrent of water. Lozen, however, raised her rifle and plunged across on her horse, inspiring the rest to cross as well, saving the group.

Another time, Lozen left the band to bring a mother and her newborn baby across the desert to the Mescalero Reservation. Afraid that gunshots would alert the Mexican and American cavalry that was patrolling the desert, Lozen killed a steer with just her knife in order to provide food for the three of them. She stole horses for the mother and herself, escaping as the bullets whizzed around her. She successfully brought the mother and child to the reservation, and thus missed the climactic battle in which Victorio and his forces were killed by Mexican troops.

Lozen supposedly could tell where the enemy was by chanting a prayer and holding her arms up. She used this power when she later fought with Geronimo's band. Lozen finally surrendered when Geronimo surrendered. She was sent as a prisoner to the hot, humid climate of Alabama. Here she died of tuberculosis sometime after 1887.

Apaches on the Great Plains hunted buffalo and used the animal not just for food, but for a variety of other things, such as clothing.

CHAPTER 4: DAILY LIFE

The Apaches ate a variety of foods. Some they hunted for, some they grew, and some they gathered.

Apaches hunted for meat, which included deer, antelope, mountain lion, and porcupine, while those on the plains followed and hunted the buffalo. Apaches who lived east of the Rio Grande, such as the Mescaleros, used the buffalo more than those west of the river in Arizona and New Mexico.

Two animals Apaches would not eat, however, were bear and fish of any type. The bear was thought to be part human, and thus off-limits. According to a Chiricahua saying, if a bear stands up on its hind legs and holds its hands up, it is trying to say that it is a friend.[1]

Fish were not eaten because they were considered relatives of the snake, which was a creature of evil. Prairie dogs and turkeys were also not eaten. After the Spanish brought other animals to the New World, the Apaches adapted to eating beef, mules, and even goats. However, they would not eat pigs because the pigs ate animals that lived around water.

Gathering food was just as necessary as hunting it. Apaches gathered prickly pears, yucca, cholla, saguaro, berries, acorns, nuts, and mesquite beans. However, the most important

Mescal was an extremely important plant to the Apaches. They cooked it and ate it as food, and often put away cooked mescal for use during the colder months when other food was scarce.

gathered food was mescal from the mescal plant. (In fact, the name of one Apache tribe—Mescalero—comes from the mescal plant.)

Mescal was harvested in late spring, such as May or June, and cooked. The males would help the females remove the head of the plant and the spiky leaves. Next a long, four-foot rock-lined pit was built. They placed the mescal in the pit and built a fire. Then the youngest child, standing to the eastern side of the pit, would throw four stones into it. The pit was covered with wet grass and clay. Finally, a rock was placed on top of the mound, and charcoal was used to draw a figure on the rock. Not only would the Apaches feast on sun-dried mescal, but it became an important food for the tribe throughout the year.

Pinion nuts and juniper berries were another important food. They would be gathered in late autumn. A single family might gather as much as 500 pounds of the nuts and berries to last them over the winter.

For drinking, Apaches made a beverage out of walnut meats, hulls, and shells. These ingredients were mashed, covered with water, and boiled. Then the liquid was strained out, leaving the pieces behind. The final product was white and tasted like milk.

Apache women wore two-piece dresses made of calico and plain, woven cloth. Their skirts were long, and they wore long blouses over the top of them. Every woman carried a knife, and some even carried guns and wore ammunition (AM-yoo-nih-shun) belts.

Warriors wore calico shirts, breechcloths made of muslin with belts to keep them from falling, and usually one or more cartridge belts. Before Apaches learned to use guns, they relied on five weapons: the bow, lance, war club, flint knife, and spear.

Apache females typically wore their hair arranged around two willow hoops worn over their ears. Some older women might have favored the Plains Apache style, which featured the hair parted in the middle and braided in two. Warriors kept their hair long, and wore headbands to keep it out of their eyes.

The hairstyles for Apache women varied depending upon age and tribe. Left to right are Brushing Against and Little Squint Eyes.

The most important piece of clothing for Apaches were their moccasins. Why? Because they often had to get off their horses and climb cliffs, either to escape enemies or to pursue animals, and trying to climb sharp rocks in bare feet was difficult, even for Apaches.[2]

Their moccasins had high tops that were pulled up when needed for warmth. These tops could also be folded below the knee for protection, such as against thorns or other sharp objects. When folded down, the moccasin served as a type of emergency kit. As an Apache said: "In those folds we carried our valuable possessions, valuable primarily in the sense of usefulness."[3] An example is extra moccasin soles (since soles wore out quickly), and the thorns of a mescal plant that were used as sewing needles to attach the new soles.

Apache moccasins, around 1860

Childbirth was important to the Apaches. However, while a pregnant woman was shown every courtesy and consideration, her condition was not allowed to interfere with her chores, and she kept right on performing her duties, sometimes to the time when she gave birth while working. During the birth, the father would leave camp, often going off to offer a prayer for the safe delivery of his child. The woman's mother, a midwife, and possibly other friends, helped with the delivery.

After a child was born, the midwife washed it in lukewarm water. Sometimes she warmed the water in her mouth and spit it on the baby. Besides warming the water, holding it in the mouth was believed to make the water helpful to the baby.[4] The baby was dried, wrapped in a soft blanket, and held up to all four directions (north, south, east, and west).

Soon after a baby was born, either its mother or maternal grandmother pierced its ears. This was believed to improve the child's ability to hear. Since Apaches were often at war, it was vital that babies keep silent, since a crying baby could endanger the rest of the band.

A baby was given a name, such as "One-Who-Laughs", but these types of names were only for children. When the child grew up, a new name was given that was more descriptive of he or she as a person. It was often impossible to tell if a child was male or female by its name.

The Apaches greatly valued names. A name was a family's special property, and usually only that family could use it. If someone else wanted to use the name, they had to get permission. On occasion, a name could be given as a gift. For example, a great warrior could promise his name to a boy he befriended. This was a very special honor, and the boy who received the name would try his hardest to be just like that warrior.

Apaches did not address each other by names. A married couple called each other "husband" and "wife", and used descriptive phrases, such as "The old man's son", when referring to others. No one chose the name of a person who had recently died. In a family, years passed before that name was used again.

Apache children were taught early on to listen to their elders. A child who was bad might have cold water thrown in his or her face, or be ignored. In a more extreme case, the child might be scared into obedience, with friends acting out the parts of evil ones who had come to drag the child off to the underworld. Using a stick on a bad child was a last resort.

When a person died, his body was dressed in his best clothes, then wrapped in a blanket and taken to the mountains, where it was thrown into a crevice (narrow opening). Occasionally, bodies were buried in small, shallow graves. The house and everything inside it that belonged to the person who passed away was burned down. Even today, Apaches who follow the traditional ways still follow this practice. This is why they live in wickiups rather than modern houses because wickiups can be rebuilt faster.[5]

A wickiup (also spelled wikiup) was another style of Apache house. Today, some Apaches who follow the traditional ways still live in wickiups.

The Evil Owl

Stories often paint owls as intelligent and all-knowing creatures. There are many in which a "wise old owl" plays a part. Even though they are sometimes shown as crabby or fussy, owls are almost always good characters.

This is not so to the Apaches.

To Apaches, owls are frightening and dangerous creatures because they represent evil spirits of dead Apaches, who return to earth to haunt the living. Owls were never used for anything by Apaches. If one was killed, it was simply discarded. The Apaches thought that just looking at owls would cause illness and twist the features of a person's face.

Owls were sometimes used to scare children. In his book about growing up as a Kiowa Apache, Jim Whitewolf talks about being threatened that an owl would take him away if he didn't go to bed. One night, Jim was being particularly naughty and his parents said that they would sing a special owl song. When he looked toward the doorway, he saw what appeared to be something with large eyes looming in it. It was actually his cousin, who had painted an owl face on a pan and was holding it in the doorway. Of course, Jim didn't know that, and such was his fear of owls that he scampered off to bed. "After that, whenever they sang that song, I went right to bed," he wrote.[6]

A famous story about owls concerns the hunt for the Apache, Geronimo, and his followers by U.S. soldiers and other Apache scouts. One of the soldiers had brought along a Great Horned Owl, and when the scouts realized it, they were terrified. It was a bad luck creature, they said, and the group had no chance of catching Geronimo as long as it was present. The soldier was forced to leave the owl behind.

Other Native-American tribes admired owls. Warriors who had proven themselves particularly brave were allowed to wear caps of owl feathers. However, to the Apaches, the owl meant only trouble.

Geronimo was an old man when this photo was taken in 1898. He is now known as the most fearsome Apache warrior, but in reality there are many others who may claim that title.

CHAPTER 5:
A PEOPLE PROVOKED

The Apaches had a reputation as a people always fighting. Did they deserve it?

Studies by researchers have shown that the Apaches were not the constant warlike demons that history and popular culture has made them out to be. The Apaches did sometimes try offering friendship, not anger, to others.

To be clear, the Apaches raided and warred with other native tribes. That sort of thing had been going on between the natives for a long time before the coming of, first the Spanish and then the Americans, to the Southwest. However, even here it does not seem that the Apaches can be constantly considered as the aggressors.

As one researcher wrote: "There is considerable evidence that the semi-nomadic Apaches cannot be branded as the initiators (the ones who start something) of all the wars of New Mexico or as the only warlike people in that area."[1]

Later he adds: "The idea of the Apaches as an essentially predatory race of Indians is probably best treated as a figment of the imagination."[2]

The Apaches initially encountered the Spanish around 1540. The natives reacted with cautious friendship upon first meeting this completely foreign people and their strange new culture. Impressed, one Spaniard said about the Apaches: "They are gentle people . . . and are faithful in their friendship."[3]

However, these initial feelings between the two sides did not last, and they were soon at war. To be sure, both sides committed terrible acts of violence against one other. Neither side was blameless. However, the Apaches were repeatedly provoked by constant kidnappings of their men, women, and children.

Even when friendship was offered, it was a trick. A Spanish governor in the late 1780s offered friendship to the natives. He then ordered the Apaches be given as much alcohol as possible so as to keep them drunk and incapable of fighting. That plan failed. Relations between the Spanish and the Apaches wore down so badly that by 1801, the Spanish governor of Santa Fe ordered the military to kill every Apache man, woman, and child that they could find.

Even when Mexico won its independence from Spain in 1822, nothing changed for the Apaches. In the 1830s, the Mexican states of Sonora and Chihuahua offered bounties (payments) for Apache scalps. This happened at the same time as more and more Americans were streaming into the Southwest looking for precious metals. The Apaches offered friendship to this new group of people, hopeful that they had found an ally against the Mexicans.[4]

Unfortunately, the results were the same for the Apaches. Lured by the scalp bounties, in 1837, a group of American trappers invited a band of friendly Apaches to a fiesta (party) at the Santa Rita copper mines in New Mexico. The trappers and Apaches mingled together, eating the food and inspecting goods to be traded. However, once the trappers slipped away, a large gun hidden in the bushes opened fire on the defenseless Apaches, killing most of them. The trappers had planned this massacre (MAH-suh-kur) (mass killing) in order to get Apache scalps and collect the payment. In revenge, the Apaches began attacking miners and travelers.

The Americans gained most of the Southwest from Mexico after the Mexican War (1846–1848), but tensions remained between them and

The Chiricahua Apaches were at peace with Americans until a U.S. Army officer tried to ambush them. Thereafter the Chiricahuas under Cochise were one of the most feared Apache tribes in the Southwest.

the natives. Yet, perhaps surprisingly, the Apaches still tried to make peace with the White-eyes. In 1861, the Chiricahua Apaches were on peaceful terms with the Americans, and some were even employed cutting wood for a stage station. The Chiricahua leaders were lured to a conference by the American military in a tent flying a white truce flag. Once there, the army tried to capture the Apaches, and a battle broke out. Some Apaches escaped, among them a chief named Cochise (KOH-cheez), who cut his way out of a tent. As a consequence, for the next ten years Cochise waged unrelenting war on the Americans, and many lives were lost.

In 1863, Apache chief Mangas Coloradas was tortured and killed by American soldiers while supposedly at a peace conference. In 1871, at Camp Grant near Tucson, Arizona, over 140 Apaches, mostly women and children, were murdered as they slept by a group of Americans, Mexicans, and other natives.

Again, both sides were at fault once violence began. The Apaches committed crimes against Americans as well, such as the Alma Massacre in April 1880, in which Apaches killed over 40 people. However, clearly the Apaches were not the only ones to blame for all the trouble.

One theory is that it was the constant kidnapping of Apache women and children drove the Apaches to hate outsiders and constantly fight

Geronimo (front center) and his men after their surrender

them. The natives knew that the boys and girls would live lives of slavery. For a culture that greatly valued its people, this was agonizing to the Apaches.

The final insult to the Apaches occurred in 1886, after the United States Army had prevailed over Native Americans throughout the country, including the Southwest. An Apache named Geronimo and his small band was one of the last to surrender. Geronimo was finally talked into giving up by Apache scouts working for the U.S. Army.

When he surrendered, Geronimo spoke words that could have applied to the whole Apache race: "Once I moved about like the wind. Now I surrender to you and that is all."[5]

Geronimo and his followers were sent to Florida as prisoners—a hot, humid place that differs greatly from the Apaches' homeland in the dry, desert climate. As their reward for trapping Geronimo, the Apache scouts were sent to Florida as prisoners too.

Today, there are thirteen Apache tribes living in the United States. There are five in Arizona, five in New Mexico, and three in Oklahoma. It is estimated that the total Apache population is about 30,000.[6] They remain a proud people, who celebrate their rich heritage while remaining active, vibrant citizens of the modern world.

Sometimes, through stories and songs either written or spoken, the old days are remembered. The days when the Apache was the undisputed lord of his domain, when he moved cat-like over the southwest desert landscape, seeing, sensing, and hearing everything, and feeling the deep-down inner peace that comes with being in perfect harmony with the world.

"They moved about freely . . . always following the sun and the food supply. They owned nothing and everything. They did as they pleased and bowed to no man."[7]

These were the Apaches. They were here first.

Cochise

Although Geronimo has become the most well-known Apache, perhaps the greatest male warrior in Apache history was Cochise.

Cochise was a Chiricahua Apache. Other Apaches called him Cheis, or oak, meaning he was strong like an oak tree.

It is thought that Cochise was born in 1805. Because he was never photographed in his life (like another famous Native American—Crazy Horse), descriptions of him have been handed down by others. They say he was about five feet, ten inches tall, and weighed about 175 pounds. He had shoulder-length dark black hair and wore three brass rings in each ear.

Cochise was likely never photographed.

For some years Cochise fought with the Spanish who had invaded his land. However, once the Americans—or White-Eyes—came, Cochise was willing to try to live in peace with them. In February 1861, he and friends and relatives came to a peace conference that a U.S. Army officer named George Bascom arranged. However, the conference was a trick, and Bascom tried to take all of the natives prisoner. Cochise cut a hole through the side of the tent in which he was imprisoned and escaped, even though he was shot in the leg. When Cochise tried to arrange for the release of his relatives, Bascom killed them. In revenge, Cochise killed the hostages he had taken, and ten years' worth of brutal warfare was underway.

Cochise proved to be a great fighter and strategist (STRAH-tuh-jist), swooping down on American and Mexican settlements and American military posts without warning. Even when the American military forced Cochise into the Dragoon Mountains in Arizona, he continued to attack the Southwest. No one slept easily with Cochise on the loose.

Finally, in 1873, with the help of a white trader named Thomas Jeffords, a truce was arranged with Cochise. He got his people a reservation that included their ancestral (an-SESS-trul) lands in the Dragoon and Chiricahua mountains, and an agreement that they could live on the reservation in any manner they chose. Thanks to Cochise, much of the Chiricahua's heritage (HAIR-ih-tij) was preserved.

Cochise died on June 8, 1874, and was buried in a secret grave whose location remains a mystery to this day.

1. Apaches used buzzard and turkey feathers for their arrows since those feathers did not wear out as fast.

2. The famous Apache, Geronimo, was not a chief. He was a medicine man and a warrior.

3. The Apaches enjoyed games and contests.

4. *Apacheria* was the name given to the lands the Apaches lived on.

5. One of the first Apache reservations was Ojo Caliente, established in 1870.

6. Apaches believed that illness could result from witchcraft or the evil actions of ghosts.

7. Women were responsible for maintaining and repairing anything needed for their homes.

8. Sometimes Apaches called horses "mystery dogs."

9. After a baby was born, it was put into a device called a cradleboard.

10. After a man and woman were married, the man would politely avoid his mother-in-law. She might even wear a bell to alert him of her presence.

Chapter One: Choosing Life

1. Elizabeth A.H. John. *Storms Brewed in Other Men's Worlds.* (Lincoln, Nebraska: University of Nebraska Press, 1975), 286.

Chapter Two: From the North

1. "Apache Indians," August, 2012, http://www.voicesofthetexashills.org/vthindians0006.htm.

2. Jeffrey D. Carlisle. *Spanish Relations with the Apache Nations East of the Rio Grande.* (Texas: University of North Texas, 2001). Accessed August, 2012, http://www.scribd.com/doc/43508263/Apaches-Del-Este.

3. "Apache Indians," August, 2012, http://www.voicesofthetexashills.org/vthindians0006.htm.

4. Alvin M. Joseph (editor-in-charge). *The American Heritage Book of Indians.* (American Heritage Publishing Co., Inc, 1961), 375.

5. Ibid, 375.

6. Elizabeth A.H. John. *Storms Brewed in Other Men's Worlds.* (Lincoln, Nebraska: University of Nebraska Press, 1975), 71.

7. Ibid, 61.

Chapter Three: Men and Women

1. Jack D. Forbes. *Apache, Navaho and Spaniard.* (Norman, Oklahoma: University of Oklahoma Press, 1960), 83.

2. Thomas E. Mails. *The People Called Apache.* (Englewood Cliffs, New Jersey: Prentice-Hall, 1974), 94.

3. Forbes, 15.

4. Jim Whitewolf. *The Life of a Kiowa Apache Indian.* (New York: Dover Publications, Inc., 1969), 62.

5. Mails, 61.

6. David Roberts. *Once They Moved Like the Wind.* (New York: Touchstone, 1993), 106.

7. "Traditional Apache Life," August 2012, http://southwestcrossroads.org/record.php?num=521.

8. http://impurplehawk.com/apache.html http://impurplehawk.com/apache.html

Chapter Four: Daily Life

1. David Roberts. *Once They Moved Like the Wind.* (New York: Touchstone, 1993), 148.

2. Bertha P. Dutton. *Indians of the American Southwest.* (Englewood Cliffs, New Jersey: Prentice-Hall, Inc., 1975), 119.

3. Ibid.

4. Thomas E. Mails. *The People Called Apache.* (Englewood Cliffs, New Jersey: Prentice-Hall, 1974), 57.

5. "Apache Indian Fact Sheet," http://www.bigorrin.org/apache_kids.htm.

6. Jim Whitewolf. The Life of a Kiowa Apache Indian. (New York: Dover Publications, Inc., 1969), 47.

Chapter Five: A People Provoked

1. Jack D. Forbes. *Apache, Navaho and Spaniard.* (Norman, Oklahoma: University of Oklahoma Press, 1960), 27.

2. Ibid, 28.

3. Ibid, 25.

4. Alvin M. Joseph. *The American Heritage Book of Indians,* editor-in-charge. American Heritage Publishing Co., Inc, 1961, 385.

5. David Roberts. *Once They Moved Like the Wind.* (New York: Touchstone, 1993), 11.

6. "Apache Indian Fact Sheet," August 2012, http://www.bigorrin.org/apache_kids.htm.

7. Bertha P. Dutton. *Indians of the American Southwest.* (Englewood Cliffs, New Jersey: Prentice-Hall, Inc., 1975), 117.

FURTHER READING

Books

Benoit, Peter. *The Apache.* Danbury, Connecticut: Children's Press, 2011.

Dwyer, Helen, and D.L. Birchfield. *Apache History and Culture.* New York: Gareth Stevens Publishing, 2012.

Jastrzembski, Joseph C. *The Apache.* New York: Chelsea House Publishers, 2011.

Kissock, Heather. *Apache.* New York: Weigl Publishers, 2010.

Mifflin, Margot. *The Blue Tattoo: The Life of Olive Oatman.* Lincoln, Nebraska: University of Nebraska Press, 2009.

Works Consulted

Capps, Benjamin, *The Indians.* Alexandria, Virginia: Time-Life Books, 1973.

Clark, La Verne Harrell. *They Sang for Horses.* The University of Arizona Press, 1966.

Dutton, Bertha P. *Indians of the American Southwest.* Englewood Cliffs, New Jersey: Prentice-Hall, Inc., 1975.

Forbes, Jack D. *Apache, Navaho and Spaniard.* Norman, Oklahoma: University of Oklahoma Press, 1960.

John, Elizabeth A.H. *Storms Brewed in Other Men's Worlds.* Lincoln, Nebraska: University of Nebraska Press, 1975.

Joseph, Alvin M. (editor-in-charge). *The American Heritage Book of Indians.* American Heritage Publishing Co., Inc., 1961.

Mails, Thomas E. *The People Called Apache.* Englewood Cliffs, New Jersey: Prentice-Hall, 1974.

Marshall, Ann. *Home: Native People in the Southwest.* Phoenix, Arizona: The Heard Museum, 2005.

Roberts, David. *Once They Moved Like the Wind.* New York: Touchstone, 1993.

Whitewolf, Jim. *The Life of a Kiowa Apache Indian.* New York: Dover Publications, Inc., 1969.

On the Internet

Apache Indian Fact Sheet

http://www.bigorrin.org/apache_kids.htm

Apache Indians

http://www.indians.org/articles/apache-indians.htmlhttp://www.indians.org/articles/apache-indians.html

Apache Indians

http://www.voicesofthetexashills.org/vthindians0006.htm

Bandera County, Texas, Historical Commission

http://www.banderacountytxhistoricalcommission.org/

Owls in Lore and Culture

http://www.owlpages.com/articles.php?section=Owl+Mythology&title=Owls+Lore+Culture&page=3

Southwest Crossroads: "Traditional Apache Life"

http://southwestcrossroads.org/record.php?num=521

SouthernNewMexico.com: "Santa Rita—The Town That Vanished Into Thin Air"

http://southernnewmexico.com/Articles/Southwest/Grant/SantaRita-Thetownthatvani.html

Texas Almanac: "Fate of Spanish Mission Changed Face of West Texas"

http://www.texasalmanac.com/topics/history/fate-spanish-mission-changed-face-west-texas-0

45

aggressor (uh-GREH-sur)—A person, nation, or group that attacks first.

barren (BEAR-in)—Flat or slightly rolling land, usually with infertile, sandy soil and few trees.

circulate (SUR-kyoo-layt)—Move or pass in a circle back to the start.

commodity (kom-MAH-dih-tee)—Something of use or value.

deceit (de-SEAT)—Cheating.

encounter—To come upon.

exterminate (eks-TERM-in-ate)—Destroy totally.

glisten (GLIH-sin)—Shine.

imitate (IH-mih-tate)—Copy.

maternal (muh-TURN-ul)—Related through the mother.

midwife—A woman who assists other women in childbirth.

muslin (MUZ-lin)—A cotton fabric of plain weave.

plunder—To rob of goods or valuables by force.

predatory (PREH-duh-tor-ee)—Preying upon others.

relentless (ree-LENT-less)—Not stopping.

retaliate (ree–TAHL-ee-ate)—Attack in return for a similar attack.

stamina (STAH-min-uh)—Physical strength.

strategist (STRAH-tuh-jist)—An expert in strategy.

torrent (TOR-int)—Water moving very fast and with great force.

versatile (VER-suh-tul)—Capable of many uses.

ABOUT THE
AUTHOR

Russell Roberts has researched, written, and published numerous books for both children and adults. Among his books for adults are *Down the Jersey Shore*, *Historical Photos of New Jersey*, and *Ten Days to A Sharper Memory*. He has written over 50 nonfiction books for children. Roberts often speaks on the subjects of his books before various groups and organizations. He lives in New Jersey.